To:

From:

D1025211

Dream Catcher

By Janet Terban Morris
Illustrated by Donna Ingemanson

PETER PAUPER PRESS, INC.
White Plains, New York

Illustrations copyright © 2002
Donna Ingemanson

Designed by Becky Terhune

Copyright © 2002
Peter Pauper Press, Inc.
202 Mamaroneck Avenue
White Plains, NY 10601
All rights reserved
ISBN 0-88088-183-6
Printed in China
14   13   12   11   10   9   8

Visit us at www.peterpauper.com

INTRODUCTION

I've dreamt in my life dreams that have stayed with me ever after, and changed my ideas: they've gone through and through me, like wine through water, and altered the color of my mind.

—EMILY BRONTË

Although you don't always realize it, you spend a portion of each night letting your unconscious spirit dance through your dreams, weaving elaborate scenes with shreds of your

past, present, and (imagined) future. When you remember these images, they may fascinate, confuse, or frighten you. "Where was I?" "Who was that person?" "What does it mean?"

From the very first documented dream in 3500 B.C. to the present day, people have been intrigued, mystified, guided, even governed by their dreams. Dreams may be fragments of

an unresolved event from the past or of subconscious desires for the present. Your spirit may be trying to rise above your current situation and move forward into the future. Dreams can wreak havoc with peaceful slumber—or bring harmony to your life.

Throughout history, the fascination with dreams has been universal. Ancient Egyptians approached dreams with religious reverence. Greek writers and philosophers including Plato and

Aristotle believed that during sleep humans and divine beings communicated, and that dreams were the memories of those conversations. Traditional Hawaiian culture teaches that during dreams, the human soul travels on journeys, meeting others and having important experiences.

Native Americans have long attached great significance to dreams and their messages. Certain tribes created *dream catchers* to filter out nightmares and retain only the best

images. According to tradition, a Lakota spiritual leader once had a vision of the wise teacher Iktomi, who appeared in the form of a spider and began to weave a web on a willow hoop. Iktomi explained that his perfectly round "web of life" would capture good dreams and visions, while letting bad dreams slip through the hole at its

center. Other native cultures describe the dream catcher as holding on to bad dreams, letting only the good ones pass through the center into consciousness. Some say a feather placed on the hoop shows the good dreams where to enter.

Early twentieth century psychiatrists Sigmund Freud and Carl Jung wrote and taught extensively about the importance of interpreting dreams. They created elaborate explanations for

each symbol in the dream traveler's repertoire.

But it is important to remember that each dreamer's journey is a personal one. Only you can decipher the meaning behind the images that appear during unconscious slumber.

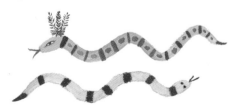

Your spirit speaks to you at night through your dreams. Listen to its messages. Use the guide to help interpret dream meanings. Learn from its images. Unravel the mysteries of your mind and sail with your creative soul on an ever sweeter dream journey.

A dream is a theatre in which the dreamer himself is the scene, the player, the prompter, the producer, the author, the public and the critic.

—CARL JUNG

Airplane

If the plane ride is exciting or pleasant it could represent the start of a new project. The experience of a plane crash could symbolize apprehension about that new project or a fear of failure.

Angel

The literal translation of "angel" is *messenger*. The angel may appear in your dream to reveal something, to comfort you, or to

fulfill a wish. Angels may also represent the goodness in you.

Arguing

May represent an actual argument
you are having in your waking hours
or may symbolize an internal struggle

that you are trying to work out. An argument in a dream may give you a way to express your feelings and release repressed anger.

Beach

Dreaming of the beach may hint at the need to slow down, relax, and take time to enjoy life. It may also be your unconscious way of fulfilling a wish to be relaxing in a sunny, pleasant paradise.

Being a Child Again

A dream of childhood could symbol- ize fond memories of happy times in

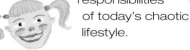

the past. It could also be an attempt to escape the responsibilities of today's chaotic lifestyle.

Being Chased

This is the most common dream among children and is second only to falling in dreams among adults. It usually means you are feeling emotional pressure from within or running away from your fears. Learning to face up to the person or thing pursuing you in your dream

usually conquers the fear and ends this type of dream.

Birth

Freud's theories on birth dreams centered on the fear or hope of becoming pregnant. Followers of Jung felt that these dreams represent the inner self or identity of the dreamer. Other dream analysts evoke a variety of meanings including hope, joy, wish-fulfillment; something the dreamer is trying to create; or a new project in development.

Car Accident

May be a warning that you are driving too fast and not paying attention! You may also be feeling out of control in some aspect of your life, or moving too fast to get ahead of the competition. A dream accident may be a warning to take precautions.

ZZZZZZ zzzzz zzzZZZ zzzz

Celebrations

Joyous celebrations usually represent a fulfilled and happy feeling of accomplishment. The type of celebration and the people sharing it with you may give clues to the deeper meaning of the dream. Or you may just be anticipating an upcoming event. A dream of disappointment may be a warning to alter your expectations.

Climbing

Whether the climb is easy or difficult, it may represent the upward course

you are embarking on. This may be an emotional, spiritual, or financial journey. Your attitude toward the climb may indicate your feelings toward the challenges ahead of you.

Color

Not everyone dreams in color. People who are more aware of color in their waking hours tend to experience multi-color dreams, while those who are less perceptive of color may see images in black and white. Particular colors may remind you of a situation from your past.

DREAM COLOR SYMBOLS

Red: passion, fire, heat, anger, danger

Yellow/Orange: sunshine, happiness, lightness, optimism; cowardice

Green: advancement (green light), nature, health, growth; jealousy (green with envy)

Blue: moody; can be uplifting and spiritual or dark and foreboding

Black: danger, depression, fear of the unknown; dark feelings

White: positive, pure, peaceful, clean; new beginnings

Crying

Crying often represents an
emotional release and letting go.
Dream crying may help to resolve
a sorrowful experience.

While awake, we think in words; asleep, we think in images.

—PATRICIA GARFIELD, Ph.D.

Dancing

Refers to the rhythm of life. Dancing expresses joy, spiritual release, and feelings of romance. As dancing represents physical relationships, dancing alone may symbolize a desire for a partner in life.

Death

Jung talked about death in dreams as a letting go of something that had

died; he felt it symbolized transformation and a new beginning. Other dream analysts feel it could have many other interpretations. Examine closely the theme of the dream to see if it may represent a need for great change in your life, a need to come to terms with death, or even a warning to take better care of yourself.

Door

An open door represents new opportunities. A closed door may represent opportunities that are not available to you. A locked or

unlocked door may reflect how
secure or insecure you are feeling in
your waking hours.

Drowning

May symbolize insecurity. You may
feel helpless about a current situation
or simply overwhelmed emotionally.

Escape

Indicates a desire to drop old ways
of seeing things, and to discover
new directions and opportunities for
your inner self.

Ex-Husband/Wife, Ex-Lover

Unresolved feelings or issues may come up in dreams of past relationships. You may be missing the companionship of the person in the dream, or you may be longing for some aspect of the person not present in yourself.

Eye

Known as the "window to the soul," the eyes when bright and open may suggest happiness and health, while closed, red, or tearful eyes signify a

need to examine your troubled soul
more closely.

Falling

Causing stress and anxiety for the
dreamer, falling may symbolize
insecurity, loss of control, or feeling
threatened. Falling may also indicate
a need to let go and trust the flow
of life.

Father

Your relationship with your father may help to interpret this dream. Your father may indicate warmth and security or strength and power, for example. Issues of discipline and structure may be brought to the surface. Dreaming of a deceased father may indicate unresolved issues or simply a sense of loss.

Fire

While Freud believed fire symbolized male power, it more often represents passion, desire, or anger. Fire may

also be a symbol of cleansing and
purifying, and may represent a desire
for a new beginning.

Fireworks

May symbolize a special occasion or
have overtones of passion and
excitement.

Flowers

Represent pleasure, relaxation, beauty, and peace. Often a symbol for the self and the heart, flowers may indicate a gesture of love. While Jung felt flowers symbolized emotions and feelings, Freud considered them to be a symbol of womanhood.

Flying

Desire for freedom, need to rise above current limitations, release of creative energy and ideas—flying dreams are one of the most

common categories.

Getting Lost
May symbolize searching for the
solution to a troubling problem.

Ghost

Appears mainly in children's dreams and may signify nighttime insecurity. In adults, a ghost may represent something or someone who is gone but not forgotten.

Grandparent

Dreaming of a grandparent may symbolize a strong bond. If the grandparent has passed on, the dream may be somewhat reassuring—it may be telling you that you have inherited some of the lost relative's traits.

*I was not looking for my dreams
to interpret my life, but rather for
my life to interpret my dreams.*

—SUSAN SONTAG

Hand

The hand may symbolize a person's
whole life. Injury to the hand may
refer to an inability to accomplish a
task or move forward.

Heaven

May signify a good mood and happy spirit. Ethereal dreams are often highly uplifting. Freud looked to heaven as a place where wishes are fulfilled, while the *I Ching* speaks of heaven as the "creative father."

Hell

Seen as a symbol for sin and ultimate punishment. You may be dealing with inner feelings of guilt. Dreams of hell are somewhat uncommon today.

Hiding

Whatever you are hiding from in your waking hours will appear to you in your dreams. As with facing your fears, if you face up to the situation, your feelings may be resolved.

Husband/Wife

Usually spouses don't appear as themselves in dreams, unless you are distanced from your spouse or are having difficulties in your relationship. A negative dream may be an early warning of problems ahead.

Ice

As with water, ice represents your emotions. Frozen water may symbolize a cold emotional state and an inability to deal with complex feelings. Skating on ice may symbolize tremulous emotions, while falling through the ice may signal a total collapse. If the ice is thawing, you could be on the verge of change.

ZZZZZZzzzzzzzz

Infidelity

May refer to the act of being unfaith-
ful or a strong desire to pursue
another in your waking life. Or, you
may feel you are not being true to an
idea or belief and may be struggling
to come to terms with your own
inconsistency.

Island

A lush and peaceful tropical island
may symbolize a need for tranquility
and solace in your life. You may be
longing for independence or simply
for change. A deserted island dream

with sad overtones may indicate loneliness or a desire to be alone, while contentment likely signals a desire for solitude.

Journey

May represent a means of escape; a way to renew and recharge your life; the road you need to travel to find your true spirit. The characters accompanying you and the places you journey to will

give clues to where this journey is leading.

Juggling

This dream of skill and balance may indicate a need to reassess priorities and slow down. Keeping all the balls in the air symbolizes your feeling of being in constant motion, while dropping the balls may signify anxiety.

Jungle

If you journey through the jungle, your dream may take on nightmarish qualities. Your fears may be personified in the dark, difficult terrain. You may also feel frustrated at trying to make your way through a wilderness labyrinth.

Kaleidoscope

Because the geometric patterns and colors are constantly moving and changing within the kaleidoscope, this dream calls out to you to add color, texture, motion (change) to your life.

Key

Keys symbolize ideas, new experiences, and inner wisdom. In a dream, the key is a message from your unconscious that you will solve a problem.

Kissing

Rarely a negative dream, kissing brings back a feeling of young love. A passionate kiss may fulfill your daytime wishes. Or you may be witness to another's kiss. If this involves your partner, it may signal a fear of infidelity. If you are about to embrace someone but wake up before the experience, you may have a feeling the kiss wouldn't be right or proper.

We need time to dream, time to remember, and time to reach the infinite. Time to be.

—GLADYS TABER

Laughter

If you wake up laughing, you begin the day's adventure in great spirits, even if the source of the dream laughter was absurd. After a long, sad spell during waking hours, a dream of laughter may lighten your mood and let you embrace life again.

Light

Jung felt that light symbolized the conscious mind. It is also a symbol of life, sunshine, exhilaration, and hope. Light represents your positive soul and creative spirit.

Lion

The lion is a symbol of bravery, strength, courage, and power. If you are fleeing a lion, examine the parts of your life or personality from which you may be running. If the lion is caged, you may be trying to over-come difficulties or you may feel trapped. In children, dreams of lions may symbolize their unconscious anger or fear.

Loss of Breath

If you have difficulty breathing from asthma, sleep apnea, or the com-

mon cold, you may experience dreams of suffocation. If there are no medical difficulties, you may be searching for more "breathing space" or freedom. You may also be too far down under the covers!

Marriage

An expression of hope for the future or wish fulfillment, dreams of marriage symbolize the joining of souls, hearts, or possibly ideas. You may be longing for partnership or struggling with commitment.

Maze

If your life has become complex and difficult, and you feel overwhelmed and confused, the dream maze may hold clues to finding your way out of your predicament.

Mirror

Jung considered it magical, Snow White found it to be prophetic, and Alice used it for her entrée into Wonderland. The reflection of another while looking into the mirror may signal living a fantasy and not facing your true identity or core issues.

Money

Your attitudes toward money are reflections of your attitudes toward sex and power. Rarely having anything to do with financial issues, a dream about money is a symbol of the ability to give and accept love.

Mother

May represent your mother and the relationship you share. May also symbolize unresolved emotions between you, or a recognition of unpleasant traits you have "inherited" from your mother. Your dreams may also represent a nurturing earth goddess—an archetypal mother figure, as in Jung's theories.

Night

Sometimes daunting, with dark overtones; may represent a fear of the unknown and apprehension about

confronting subconscious issues.

Nightingale

As with most winged creatures, the nightingale may represent your aspirations, embarking on optimistic goals, or your soul's desire to soar to spiritual freedom.

Nightmares

Stress, anxiety, life-changes, or physical ailments may lead young and old to experience distressing and often terrifying nightmares. This type of dream is more harrowing than an

ordinary bad dream. By facing the feared person or situation, you diffuse its power and its hold over you. You can actually learn to change the outcome of your dream. This is very useful if you have recurrent nightmares.

Nudity

This extremely common dream deals with embarrassment, shame, or feeling over-exposed.

In forming a bridge between body and mind, dreams may be used as a springboard from which man can leap to new realms of experience lying outside his normal state of consciousness and enlarge his vision not only of himself, but also of the universe in which he lives.

—ANN FARADAY

Ocean

Water represents emotions and emotional energy. Jung thought of the ocean as a symbol of the unconscious and a place of creativity and fertility. Your personal connection to the ocean may yield a more nuanced interpretation.

Octopus

May symbolize business dealings, entanglements, or having too many activities going on at the same time.

Owl

Represents wisdom and knowledge. Owls have the ability to see in the dark and may represent your inner wisdom.

Panic

Heart-racing panic may occur in dreams, causing you to wake suddenly with a feeling of great distress. Usually related to nightmares, dream panic may be a reflection of fears and anxieties in your waking life.

Path

The context of this dream is the most important aspect. If your path is smooth and without obstacles, you may be happy with the direction you are traveling in life. If the path is rocky, with roadblocks and difficult terrain, you may need to rethink recent key decisions.

Performing

Relates to your personality and how you want to appear to others. You may be looking for acceptance and recognition if your performance is successful. A dream of performing badly or forgetting your lines may indicate a demanding schedule, a lack of self-confidence, or a feeling of inadequacy.

Public Speaking

Studies show that the fear of speaking in public is the number one fear, so it is relatively common in dreams.

If you are dressed inappropriately or not at all, you may fear being scrutinized or exposed in some way.

Quarrel

Symbolizing an inner conflict, this dream may have more to do with opposing sides of your personality searching for balance than an actual argument with another.

Quicksand

Signifies insecurity and emotional upheaval. If you wake up with a "sinking" feeling, you will need to address feelings of being bogged down, pulled down, or held down in your current situation.

It is in our idleness, in our dreams, that the submerged truth sometimes comes to the top.

—*VIRGINIA WOOLF*

Rain

Rain has a strong association with your emotions and may relate to a need for emotional or spiritual cleansing. The  context and intensity of the rainfall is significant. Light drizzle is less serious than downpours and hail.

Rainbow

A symbol of sun and water— fire and rain—a rainbow is almost always a positive sign of blessing, success, and completeness.

Rejection

Signifies insecure feelings and a fear of not being accepted.

Ring

Representing wholeness, commitment, and marriage, the ring is a positive symbol. As a circle with no beginning and no end, it may also symbolize immortality.

Rollercoaster

May be a sign that you feel your life is out of control. Your emotions are soaring upward and careening

downward at the same time.

Rose

A symbol of love, courage, comfort, and devotion, the rose evokes feelings of pleasure and reassurance.

Running

Your pace in the dream has a great deal to do with the pace of your life. If you are taking a slow jog, you may feel somewhat satisfied. If you are being chased or if you are trying to flee a frightening situation, consider

the stresses in your life. An inability to run may signify feeling paralyzed and unable to take a meaningful step forward.

Searching

An extremely frustrating dream. Searching endlessly for a missing person, place, or thing parallels a search for clarity in your waking hours. The outcome of the dream is important to its meaning. Consider as well the people who may have helped you find what was missing.

Serpents and Snakes

Because they can't close their eyes, snakes symbolize wisdom and

awareness. Constantly shedding their skins, they represent transformation and rebirth. Serpents and snakes inspire fear and curiosity.

Women dream of snakes as often as men do.

Singing

A beautiful melody sung in harmony may symbolize balance of spirit and meaningful relationships in your waking life. If your song is discordant and off key, it may reveal a problem in communicating.

Slow Motion

Similar to frustrating dreams of being chased or running and not getting anywhere, this dream relates to

anxiety, frustration, and fears. It may represent a need to distance your-self from a person or place, or a need to let go of ineffective ideas and troubling emotions.

Spider

Constantly busy spinning elaborate webs, the spider may symbolize your artistic and productive side. It may be time to begin a new creative project or find more interesting pursuits.

Sun

Jung felt that the sun represents the conscious mind. It is the creative center, the source of energy and vitality. The sun rising may represent new beginnings and positive attitudes at the start of a new journey. A romantic sunset with a loved one may represent wish-fulfillment fantasies.

Swan

Thought of as a messenger, the swan is also a symbol of family and togetherness. While powerful and strong in the water, the swan radiates dignity and grace. May be a metaphor for women today.

An uninterpreted dream is like an unopened letter from God.

—THE TALMUD

Teeth

One of the most common anxiety dream themes, loss of teeth usually refers to "losing face" and other

concerns with self-image. In a less common interpretation, the dream suggests speaking out of turn or a need to keep your mouth shut. A toothache in a dream is sometimes

an early warning of dental problems, and you may want to schedule an appointment with your dentist.

Test-Taking

Freud believed that test-taking dreams occurred just before facing a challenge or an occasion when the dreamer has to perform well. Fear of failure is a common theme in these dreams, where the subject feels unprepared for the exam, can't find the room where the exam is taking place, or has suddenly forgotten everything she needs to know or do.

This anxiety dream may lead you to probe your insecurities and to think about how to better prepare yourself for career and life challenges.

Thirst

May signify a longing for something missing in your waking life. You may have needs and desires not being met. If upon waking you really are thirsty, the dream may simply indicate you need a drink of water!

Tightrope

If you are having a marvelous time balancing, performing, and entertaining others, this dream may symbolize a need for more pleasure and enjoyment in life. If you are teetering on the high wire or if you fall from above, you may be anxious about risk-taking.

Unable to Call for Help

A feeling of being threatened, powerless, or trapped is usually a reflection of current experiences in your life. Calling out for help and remaining unheard is not only

frustrating, but could be damaging to your spirit.

Undressing

May indicate a need to be more open and expose your true self to the world. You may have a desire to be freer and enjoy a less constricting life.

ZZZZZZZZZZZZZZZZZZZZZ

Unicorn

An ancient symbol of hope and purity, the unicorn is a gentle animal that wooed his virgin by placing his head in her lap. Jung saw the unicorn as the symbol of the self. It also may represent the fantasy world and a need for escape from the stresses of reality.

Unlocked Doors and Windows

Intimidating, even threatening, the finding of open doors and windows in your dream is a direct reflection of

insecurity in your waking life. You may need to reassess your sense of self and work to build a stronger foundation for emotional well being.

Victory

Symbolizes the need to compete and succeed. You may be struggling with an internal conflict that needs resolution.

Voice (or Lack of)

See Unable to Call for Help.

Water

Suggesting a feeling of floating peacefully in the womb, water dreams are among the most comforting and relaxing dreams you may experience. Often a reflection of your emotional state, the water may represent "going with the flow." Taoists believe that water is the essence of life. Also see Ice, Ocean, and Rain.

Waterfall

Rushing water, and being swept along with it, may symbolize your attitudes toward the process of birth.

Window

Freud felt that the house represented the body and the windows symbolized the eyes. Take a closer look at the windows in your dream to observe the outside world, as Jung suggests. You may find symbols in either the murkiness or clarity of your windows.

Wings

Your spirit wants to ascend to greater heights. This common dream may lift your soul and challenge you to do more, be more, and feel more.

Working

Dreams of work and being in constant motion may extend the stresses of the day into what should be peaceful slumber. They symbolize unresolved issues in your work life or with life in general. They may also provide a way to work through emotional problems.

Yacht

May symbolize wealth, riches, pampered personalities, or the desire for a spiritual journey.

Youth

Celebrating simpler times, nostalgic dreams bring you back to your youth, capturing positive feelings and images to hold with you now. You may find lost optimism and compassion or regain a more enthusiastic attitude.

Zoo

You may be searching for your animal side, or more playful traits that will free your spirit. Caged animals in your dream may signify a need to let go and run free.

Yet keep within your heart
A place apart
Where little dreams may go,
May thrive and grow.
Hold fast—hold fast your dreams!

—LOUSE DRISCOLL